THE
SALES EXCELLENC
POCKETBOOK

C000186186

By Patrick Forsyth
Drawings by Phil Hailstone

"Thoroughly entertaining, thoughtful and well-presented. Will encourage would-be salespeople to view selling in a different light."
David Horchover, Principal, Chase International Marketing

"I have read several of Patrick's books but I must say this is probably the best. Invest just an hour in reading this book and you will find a mine of practical advice, usable from day one."
Phillippa Bourne, Head of Non-Accredited Programmes, The Institute of Management

Published by:
Management Pocketbooks Ltd
Laurel House, Station Approach, Alresford, Hants SO24 9JH, U.K.
Tel: +44 (0)1962 735573   Fax: +44 (0)1962 733637
E-mail: sales@pocketbook.co.uk
Website: www.pocketbook.co.uk

This edition published 1998.   Reprinted 1999, 2000, 2003, 2004, 2005.

© Patrick Forsyth 1998

ISBN 1 870471 57 1

British Library Cataloguing-in-Publication Data – A catalogue record for this book
is available from the British Library.

Design, typesetting and graphics by **efex ltd**.   Printed in U.K.

CONTENTS

**Key techniques to maximise the effectiveness
of sales meetings:**

INTRODUCTION

"God is on the side not of the heavy battalions, but of the best shots"

Voltaire

INTRODUCTION

THE ROLE OF SELLING

Selling is as much a part of an organisation's marketing armoury as advertising, promotion or any other technique.

Often, selling is the final link in a long chain of contacts an organisation makes with its market:

- Public relations
- Press relations
- Advertising
- Direct mail
- Sales promotion (competitions, sponsorship, brochures, web sites, newsletters, exhibitions, etc)

All these may increase awareness and interest, moving a prospect nearer to the point of decision and purchase.

Usually, only the personal, face-to-face, often one-to-one contact between the customer and a salesperson actually produces business.

Selling is a vital catalyst to the process of successful business.

THE CHALLENGE

It is said that selling was never easy and that, in today's increasingly competitive markets, it is downright difficult.

The **marketing mix** - the three **P**s - describes the variables any organisation must work with in relating to its marketplace:

- **Product** (or service)
- **Price**
- **Presentation** (everything that contributes to persuasive communication, from advertising to sales promotion, from personal selling to customer care)

Look at what you sell from your customers' point of view. They have plenty of choice, certainly with regard to products or services that are themselves similar and which are similarly priced.

It is the third **P** that now differentiates (or does not) - **it is how you sell that makes the difference.**

INTRODUCTION

THE CHALLENGE

Of course, many things contribute
to the likelihood of sales success,
not least the quality of the product or
service itself.

But the 'commodity'
factor of everything appearing
(superficially at least) very similar
means that the people doing the
selling are disproportionately
important.

Where people do nothing to
differentiate - 'the bland leading
the bland' - sales go by default.

THE OPPORTUNITY

When one potential supplier
stands out then it really helps
the making of the buying decision.

It is not, of course, a
question of gimmicks.
The illustration right indicates
the **degree** of perceived
difference that it is
possible to create,
not the **manner**
of that difference.

Remember the old saying:
'You do not have to be different to be good, being
good can be different enough'. And 'good' is what potential customers define it to be.

A PROFESSIONAL APPROACH

What makes customers say of some suppliers: 'They are good people to do business with'? If we say the answer is 'to be professional' we must define what that means; or rather discover what our customers mean by it.

To be regarded as professional, salespeople must be:

- Knowledgeable (of customers and their needs, of the product/service sold and of the industry and technical area involved)
- Empathic (visibly able to put themselves in the customers' shoes)
- Confident
- Expert
- Able to offer good advice
- Sincerely interested in the customer
- Consistently reliable
- Able to create an appropriate business relationship
- Flexible, able to tailor their approach to the individual
- Visibly well prepared and organised

And more, no doubt.

Notice that all these are factors that you can **actively** aim to include, and perhaps emphasise, in your chosen approach.

THE SALES TASK

In modern competitive markets, selling has a multifaceted task to achieve. It must:

- **Communicate:** imparting information and creating awareness
- **Persuade:** showing that your offering is inherently desirable
- **Differentiate:** creating a difference between you, and your product/service, and competition

Sales techniques must address all three aspects of the task.

UNDERSTANDING CUSTOMERS

Selling is not something you 'do to people'; it has more in common with shaking them by the hand than punching them on the nose.

Definition: selling is well described as 'helping people make buying decisions'. Seen thus, it is less adversarial and, approached thus, it is more likely to be acceptable.

Few will respond to 'pushy' salespeople who think only of themselves and of making the sale and the financial reward.

Successful selling means understanding what customers are trying to do, and helping them make decisions they consider sensible.

UNDERSTANDING CUSTOMERS

And what are customers trying to do? They want to make considered decisions, ones they do not look back on and regret.

They 'weigh up' the case
put to them and only
buy when the positive
picture it describes swings
the balance convincingly.

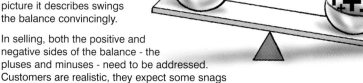

In selling, both the positive and
negative sides of the balance - the
pluses and minuses - need to be addressed.
Customers are realistic, they expect some snags
(after all when did you last buy something that was perfect?).

The successful salesperson paints a picture of a positive balance - one that stacks up better than any other described by competition.

UNDERSTANDING CUSTOMERS

Because of the attitude customers take and the competitive nature of the market place, the sales process is inherently **fragile**. In other words, small factors in how things are done can make the difference between success and failure.

One more well chosen word, appropriate description or added detail can win the order.

One less plus on the balance, or something that allows too much to mount up on the minus side, can lose the order.

Successful salespeople give attention to the detail that creates a positive difference.

THE FUNDAMENTAL SKILLS

All salespeople need to deploy a triple combination of skills that blend into a persuasive approach:

- **Service:** this is paramount; everything from being prompt for a meeting to ensuring reliable after-sales service matters
- **Technical excellence:** for instance, in product knowledge; nothing but 100% proficiency will do here (anything less will be noticed and will dilute effectiveness)
- **Sales skill:** the detail of the many techniques that contribute to a persuasive approach must be **actively** built into your approach

Remember, three legged stools fall over whichever of their legs is weak.

THE FUNDAMENTAL SKILLS

Another core element of any successful approach is **tailoring**. This means that what a salesperson does **must** be seen to be directed at an individual.

Customers hate being treated as customers. They think of themselves as individuals; they **are** individuals. Everything that makes them feel that they are not getting the 'standard spiel', but instead are having everything related to them and their unique situation, builds the chances of a positive response.

Just one 'you' phrase (eg: 'knowing the tight deadline **you** are working to, I have...') can increase acceptance of what follows.

Successful salespeople are adept at tailoring their approach, customer by customer.

THE SUCCESS FACTORS

Four key factors influence the chances of sales success:

1. **Who you see**
2. **How many people you see**
3. **How often you see them (frequency of contact)**
4. **The quality of technique used to communicate with them**

Three of the four are concerned with **sales productivity:**
essentially, if you select the best prospects, see
more of them rather than less, and keep in
regular touch with those who need it, then
sales will be higher.

In part, sales success is a numbers game:
the more quality sales meetings
(or contacts) you have, the more
you will sell.

FUTURE APPROACHES

There are no 'magic formulae' in selling; success goes to those who are concerned about the detail and select and deploy the appropriate approach day by day, meeting by meeting, customer by customer.

Selling is dynamic. There is no one right way that is valid for ever. Successful sales-people spend a lifetime fine-tuning their approach to make sure it brings the best results today - and tomorrow.

Sales excellence is the cumulation of concern for the details, which results in a fluid, fluent conversation that works for the customer.

THE RESULTS

An intelligent, considered approach can ensure:

- Identification of the **best prospects**
- **Maximum strike rate** of 'YESs' to 'NOs' (though realistically remember that there will always be some 'NOs')
- The greatest possible **sales revenue** (and profitability*)
- Creation of business relationships that ensure that customers are held, developed and that most come back and buy regularly

None of this 'just happens'; successful salespeople work at creating sales success, through all the details that create sales excellence.

* This may also be a matter of the deal, and financial arrangements, struck: see my book 'The Negotiator's Pocketbook' in this same series.

BEFORE THE SALES MEETING

LAYING THE FOUNDATIONS OF SUCCESS

There is an old saying, originating in wartime, that 'time spent in reconnaissance is seldom wasted'. In wartime it reduced the chances of getting shot. In selling, it may not be the most exciting part of the job to tie down certain basics **before** speaking to a prospect, but it can easily make the difference between a 'yes' and a 'no'.

Sales excellence comes, in part, from careful groundwork.

"You're well informed; yes let's meet"

PROSPECTING

Most businesses need the life blood of new prospects; whether you need a few occasionally, or many on a regular basis, finding enough - and finding appropriate ones - is a matter of some importance.

Some prospects come through promotional activity, others - perhaps the majority - must be found by salespeople as part of their core tasks.

Some people avoid prospecting because of a distaste for 'cold calling'. The trick is to adopt the right attitude - some see opportunities everywhere - and make obtaining new prospects a matter of system and routine.

The age old question: 'Is the glass half empty, or half full?'

PROSPECTING

EXAMPLES

Here are a few examples of methods that can create new business contacts on an ongoing basis:

- **Endless chain:** making one thing lead to another, by <u>asking</u>: 'Do you know anyone else who might be interested ...?'; by <u>analysing</u>: 'If this banker is interested, which others can I contact?'
- **Centres of influence:** these are contacts who, while they might be customers themselves, can recommend others (eg: a trade association or professional body)
- **Personal observation:** keep your eyes open, opportunities are all around; watch the trade press, find out who is moving into those new offices you drive past every day, walk downstairs in office blocks and see who else is on other floors
- **Chance contacts:** all sorts of people might be potential customers, eg: on a plane, find out who you are sitting next to (a good opening is to ask how much they paid for their ticket!)
- **Cold canvass:** knocking, uninvited, on doors hardly ever has a good rate of strike, but it may be a good way of discovering, from a receptionist, the buyer's name - making a second contact later more likely to be useful

PROSPECTING

EXAMPLES (Cont'd)

- **Lists:** there are a host of sources of names, everything from 'Yellow Pages' to association membership lists or interest groups, and directories of all sorts

- **Past customers:** go back to a dormant customer, who may only be not buying out of neglect (a good tactic when you are new to a company; ask who have others given up on?)

- **Suppliers:** look at who your organisation does business with (there is probably an A-Z list in accounts) and consider whether there are any potential customers here; they are likely to give you a hearing

- **Extra curricular activities:** it is worth analysing what committees you should sit on, what conferences you should attend, etc; share the list you produce with colleagues to make actioning it manageable

Sales excellence is enhanced by a systematic approach to prospecting; find the approaches that work for you, action them, and give it regular time.

PROSPECTING

LOOK FOR THE GREATEST POTENTIAL

Some prospects are more likely to be converted than others.

Match the criteria that make for the best prospects in your business against the names you identify, separate the wheat from the chaff, and go for those with the greatest potential.

Check such factors as the kind of organisation, the size, ownership, the level of the decision maker and the financial status (remember the old adage: 'It is not a sale until the money is in the bank'; customers must be able and willing to pay). Now prioritise those that best meet the criteria you set.

Sales excellence includes spending the most time on the best, that is qualified, prospects.

PROSPECTING

IDENTIFYING THE TRUE BUYER

Increasingly, buying decisions are made by groups of people, committees, the Board, two people in concert. It is not always clear who 'the buyer' is. A well known mnemonic tells us to look for the **MAN** who has the:

Money
Authority
Need

You might usefully categorise people into the following groups:

- Decision makers
- Advisors
- Users
- Gatekeepers
- Administrators

Deal with each in a different way as necessary.

PROSPECTING

IDENTIFYING THE TRUE BUYER

An example illustrates the various categories of people you are likely to deal with:

The Managing Director (<u>decision maker</u>) asks his Office Manager (<u>advisor</u>) to check out possible new fax machines. He involves his Secretary (<u>user</u>) in meetings because she uses such a machine much more than he does personally. Telephone calls are made via the Switchboard Operator (<u>gatekeeper</u>) who can deny or allow salespeople access to others. Finally, the order - and order number, etc - is issued by the purchasing department (<u>administrator</u>).

The process of identifying who you are dealing with and how the customer is organised starts before the meeting, but may continue throughout the sales process.

BEFORE THE SALES MEETING

BE PREPARED

'Engage the brain before the mouth' - an old but wise premise.

The best sales meetings are those that take place as the result of some thought.

The key rules of preparation are:

- **Always** do it
- Do any necessary research thoroughly
- Set clear objectives
- Work out the 'shape' of the meeting you intend to run
- Organise any support elements (eg: visual aids)
- Remain flexible thereafter (planning should create a route map, not a strait-jacket)

Sales excellence is much more likely if you 'do your homework'

BEFORE THE SALES MEETING

BE PREPARED - 3 KEY ELEMENTS

1. RESEARCH

Planning may take the form of either just a few minutes' thought and perhaps making a few notes before you go into a meeting, or an hour or two round a table thrashing out the best approach with some colleagues. Research is a key element of the process.

Find out something about the people you plan to meet.

As well as the basic details of the organisation and its business, check out (in the trade press, in the firm's annual report or web site, etc) such things as current developments/problems, its market or even just the atmosphere of an organisation (eg: ask the receptionist as you wait 'What's it like working here?').

Obtaining such information, and letting the fact that you have done so show - 'I noticed the big order you have just got from Europe mentioned in the trade press' - **can be invaluable to making a meeting go well.**

BEFORE THE SALES MEETING

BE PREPARED - 3 KEY ELEMENTS

2. SET CLEAR OBJECTIVES

Just aiming to sell 'as much as possible' is no help in deciding <u>how</u> to go about it. Sales objectives, to quote a much used mnemonic, should be **SMART**:

Specific   Setting out clearly what you intend

Measurable   Being specific tends to make objectives measurable; put in some numbers

Achievable   Is it something a customer would reasonably agree to or are you aiming impossibly high?

Realistic   <u>Should</u> you aim for it? (eg: it is no good aiming to meet a deadline which Production would find impossible to meet)

Timed   <u>When</u> are you aiming to see results? At the end of the meeting, in 6 weeks, in 6 months?

Clear objectives act to create and direct the kind of meeting you want and can make work.

BE PREPARED - 3 KEY ELEMENTS

3. SUPPORT ELEMENTS

To paint a picture as you sell, use charts, graphs (especially to present financial information clearly), photographs, brochures, samples, examples, cases - consider and utilise anything and everything that may help to strengthen the case you put.

Make sure that:

- You have the right things with you
- You can locate specifics promptly
- It all looks organised
- Some elements are (apparently) personalised (ie: do not say 'Let me show you ....', rather: 'I thought a graph might explain this more easily, so I prepared this for you to look at')

In selling, remember a picture may really be worth a thousand words.

CUSTOMER RECORDS

Many salespeople regard keeping sales records as a chore; BIG mistake! **Good, clear sales records are invaluable as one of the elements directing action,** especially with customers who are seen regularly.

So, do not trust your memory (can you really claim to be able to remember every tiny detail about perhaps hundreds of contacts?).

Keep records and keep them up to date, recording everything that may help your <u>next</u> contact with them.

Records should save time, ensure accuracy and their use should add positively to the usefulness of your preparation.

CUSTOMER RECORDS

Information which can be recorded suggests 5 main categories:

1. **Basic details** (such as names, addresses and everything from fax numbers to account numbers)
2. **Business details** (such as planned developments, when their financial year runs, etc)
3. **Personal details of contacts** (from birthdays to interests, preferences and prejudices)
4. **Logistical details** (such as the best place to park)
5. **Record of business** (such as what has been sold and its value)

Remember: your responsibility is to keep records for your organisation not yourself; one day you are not going to be there and someone else will have to take them over. Is your random scribble really good enough?

MAKING THE RIGHT INITIAL IMPRESSION

The next sections all deal with 'key techniques to maximise the effectiveness of sales meetings'

MAKING THE RIGHT INITIAL IMPRESSION

MANNER

The archetypal image of the salesperson is not entirely flattering; words such as pushy, self-centred and even dishonest come to mind and make customers wary.

Adopting the right manner can differentiate you from the stereotype, help get things off to a good start and act positively for you throughout the meeting.

So, always:

- Be conscious of the manner you adopt
- Make sure you appear professional
- Tailor your approach to the customer (eg: respond to the customer's need for you not to waste time, to give particular attention to detail, to spell out clearly, say, a financial justification, etc)

Emphasise those elements of your approach that will be most appreciated by the buyer.

CREATING INTEREST

You will never sell anything unless people want to hear what you have to say; and you need to persuade them of that.

Imagine what the customer is thinking early on ('Is this going to be useful? Am I wasting my time?') and aim to get the person responding positively even in the first moments ('This seems as if it will be useful. So far so good. Let's see what they have to say'.).

So, make sure you:

- Appear well organised
- Suggest an agenda that makes sense to the customer
- Clear, if necessary, how long the meeting can last
- Get promptly down to business

And, above all, make it clear that what you intend is designed to be right for the customer, not just for you.

A genuine, and visible, interest in the customer is a good foundation for all that must be done in the first moments.

DIRECTING THE MEETING

As Shakespeare put it in *Much ado about nothing*: '...an two men ride of a horse, one must ride behind'.

So too with meetings; when two parties meet one tends to lead, the other to follow. **When you wear the 'sales hat' you must see the meeting as yours.**

What are the rules here?

- Start off in charge and stay in charge
- Take the initiative
- Lead the meeting
- Remember this does not necessarily mean doing most of the talking and certainly does not mean coming over as pushy
- Make the customers feel that what is happening is natural, right and best for them

Run the kind of meeting <u>you</u> want, and which they find <u>they</u> like (and preferably like better than their dealings with your competitors).

DISCOVERING CUSTOMER NEEDS

DISCOVERING CUSTOMER NEEDS

A DEFINING MOMENT

To say that this is a key stage is to risk serious understatement.

Two factors are key here:

1. **If you find out more, and more thoroughly, what a customer wants (and why) than a competitor, then everything else you do can be better directed and is more likely to succeed.**

2. **Conversely, if the finding out process is skimped or inaccurately conducted compared with a competitor, everything else you do is going to be more difficult and stands less chance of success.**

Moral: take care to identify customers' needs.

DISCOVERING CUSTOMER NEEDS

QUESTIONING TECHNIQUES

The precision with which questions are asked is important. Always:

- Seek permission to ask questions and make the necessity for it clear (essentially to enable you to help them)

- Avoid any possibility of ambiguity and phrase questions clearly

- Use a series of questions to probe, digging at the same area to obtain more detail, clarification, or the reasons behind initial answers

- Ask 'open' questions to get people talking

- Take notes (it is a courtesy to ask permission)

- Organise sufficient time for this process and justify it in customer terms

QUESTIONING TECHNIQUES

GETTING PEOPLE TALKING

'Open' questions deserve a further word. By definition, open questions cannot be answered by 'Yes' or 'No'; they therefore avoid monologue and get people talking.

The best lead-ins are:

1. Kipling's 'six honest serving men':
   - what
   - why
   - where
   - when
   - who
   - how

2. The magic phrase: "Tell me about ......"
   And sometimes: "Tell me **more** about ......"

Remember: most people enjoy nothing more than talking about themselves and what is important to them; they <u>want</u> you to understand their situation.

THE IMPORTANCE OF LISTENING

Good salespeople are good listeners. Customers want to deal with people who take an interest and with whom they can relate.

Remember the old saying about people being designed with two ears and one mouth for a good reason.

But bear in mind also that listening is an **active** process, and that you must be **seen** to be a good listener.

ACTIVE LISTENING

If it is to have full effect, listening must be seen as something that needs working at.

Keys to active listening are to:

● Listen carefully; and check immediately if something is not clear

● Concentrate (ie: focus on what is being said rather than on what you plan to say next)

● Augment your memory with good note taking, especially regarding key points

● Look like a good listener; focus your attention visibly on the other person and acknowledge information as you go: 'right ... good ... got that'

Active listening will help you take in more, miss less and, ultimately, convince the customer that you understand what is wanted.

DISCOVERING CUSTOMER NEEDS

AGREEING NEEDS

Questioning is not solely a matter of probing for information and making a mental note of what is given.

It must be made entirely clear to customers that you do understand. Why should they accept suggestions or recommendations you make later if they do not think they are made in a way that relates to an understanding of their needs?

Needs can be agreed by:

- Acknowledging them: 'Right, I understand'
- Restating them: 'Yes ... so hitting this deadline really is paramount'

Always create the unmistakable view that you are totally appreciative of the customer's point of view.

ORDERING PRIORITIES

Customers often appear to have more than one priority. They say things like: 'I must have it ready by the end of May, costing no more than last time and installation must not hinder existing operations'.

This can create a dilemma for the supplier. For example, something may be able to be done quicker but, if so, higher costs may be unavoidable.

Some questions should, therefore, be directed at ordering those priorities that are listed as if equal.

Once you know, for example, that timing is so important that costs take second place, you can deal with the matter on the customer's terms: 'Now, you did say this question of timing was the most important ....'

DISCOVERING CUSTOMER NEEDS

THE EFFECT

A final point here: the power of questioning is completely wasted if it makes no difference to what is done next. If you ask lots of questions then simply leave the answers on one side and seem to give 'the standard spiel', your credibility will take a dive.

The answers to your questions must act as the fine-tuning for how - exactly, how - you proceed through the next stage: that of presenting your case.

THE EFFECT

Successful salespeople refer to
and use the information
throughout the meeting
so that it is apparent to the
customer that they are so doing.

PRESENTING THE BEST CASE

THE BUSINESS FOCUS

Any sales meeting is a meeting between two people and it would be a dull old world if when people met there was no chat. Any meeting has an informal content and this is necessary, in part ritual (how often in the UK do we chat pointlessly about the weather?), and contributes to the overall feeling and success of the meeting.

But ...... be careful.

Most customers are busy. They value their time, and they appreciate you valuing it too.

Thus there is a fine line between a level of informality that makes you regarded as pleasant to do business with, and being labelled as a time-waster.

THE KEY OBJECTIVES

If a truly **persuasive** case is to be presented, aim to make what you say:

- **Understandable**
- **Attractive**
- **Credible**

The achievement of all three objectives
blends what you say into the best
possible case; all are equally important
and all need separate consideration.

**It is here in the heartland of the sales
meeting that the detail of what is done
can progressively differentiate you from
the competition until there is only one decision
possible for the customer: choosing you.**

MAKING IT UNDERSTANDABLE

Communication can too easily be taken for granted. Yet, it is inherently difficult and misunderstandings occur all too easily. Even the simplest exchange can end with people saying 'What do you mean?' or not saying it and simply remaining confused.

Remember the phrase attributed to the late U.S. President Nixon:

> *I know that you understand what you think I said, but I am not sure you realise that what you heard is not what I meant.*

All clear?

48

PRESENTING THE BEST CASE

MAKING IT UNDERSTANDABLE

IMPORTANCE OF CLARITY

Psychologists refer to what they call **cognitive cost**. This describes the perceived level of difficulty something seems to present (eg: for the older generation, opening at random an instruction book for a video recorder or other electrical appliance finds a page that shouts out: 'This is going to be difficult!').

Conversely, people warm quickly to anything (or anyone) that makes easy what they expect is going to be hard.

Because of this, **clarity of description or explanation presents a very real opportunity to build the strength of your case;** some thought in this area can separate you positively from your competitors.

Exceptional clarity is the best foundation for all other sales description.

PRESENTING THE BEST CASE

MAKING IT UNDERSTANDABLE

A MAJOR DANGER

Customers are only human. They have normal feelings and one of these is that they do not like to look stupid.

This means that customers will frequently not respond to something that is unclear. They will avoid saying 'Hang on, I don't understand' for fear of appearing foolish when it is assumed that they should understand.

It is, therefore, very important to achieve good understanding first time. Otherwise the case you make may become progressively diluted in effectiveness as the customer fails to understand and see the full picture.

PRESENTING THE BEST CASE

MAKING IT UNDERSTANDABLE
THE RULE FOR CLARITY

Always:

- Think about explanations and descriptions, try them out, be sure they give the right information and give them with certainty

- Aim to make what you say immediately and easily understandable (take note of any clarifying questions and ask yourself if you could get your message across with another, clearer, form of words)

- Make explanations thorough and precise, telling people what they want to know and going into an appropriate level of detail

- Match the level of technicality to individual buyers, depending on their knowledge and experience

- Avoid excessive use of jargon (and match it to the circumstances)

PRESENTING THE BEST CASE

MAKING IT UNDERSTANDABLE

USE OF JARGON

Jargon is professional slang, and there is nothing wrong in saying 'I recommend model X356, from our modular range, inclusive of parts 76A and 78B and up-rated ESO' if people will understand. But will they? What you might say to a colleague will not always be understood by a customer who will think you uncaring or stupid and resent having to ask what you mean.

So, avoid excessiveness in these areas:

- **Internal jargon** (eg: abbreviations of product details, departments or systems)
- **Industry jargon** (ie: the technical jargon of a specialist field; getting the level right is most important here)
- **General phraseology** (be very sure both parties interpret a word like 'immediately' the same way or you could have problems)
- **Technical jargon** (for instance, do not say you will send something as a pdf file unless you are sure it will be understood)

MAKING IT ATTRACTIVE

People do not buy products or services, they buy what they do for them.

This is the key principle of this stage of the sales process. As such, you must be able to differentiate between, and work with, what are called **features** and **benefits**:

- A **feature** is what a product/service, or a part/element of it, is

- A **benefit** is what a product/service does for, or means to, a customer

Customers are best persuaded by a style of selling which 'talks benefits'.

FEATURE   **BENEFIT**

MAKING IT ATTRACTIVE

BENEFITS AND FEATURES

Benefits are most important to customers, but features are what make these possible, making their mention important too.

Example

A car has many features. One such might be a 5-speed gearbox. There are several benefits conferred on the customer by this: greater fuel economy (than a 4-speed or automatic gearbox), quieter running at high speed, and less wear and tear on the engine at high speeds.

Any statement about, in this case, the car can be analysed just by asking what something means. Thus: quieter running = less distraction/tiredness = better concentration = greater safety (which is a benefit).

Putting benefits first as you lay out the facts links most strongly to customer needs: 'For best fuel economy and lowest running cost, the model with the 5-speed gearbox makes better sense'.

MAKING IT ATTRACTIVE

BENEFITS AND FEATURES (Cont'd)

While benefits and features are definitive statements about a product or service, a benefit is only useful if it matches the customer and the customer's needs.

Example
Fuel economy arising from a car's 5-speed gearbox is only useful if the customer is concerned about it (if you are selling something like a Porsche, then it probably is not!).

A benefit is only useful if it matches the needs of an individual customer.

MAKING IT ATTRACTIVE

BENEFITS AND FEATURES (Cont'd)

Benefits come in various 'varieties', such as:

- Benefits related to the customer's job (specifically in business to business selling)
- Benefits to the customer as a person
- Benefits to other people important to the customer

Example

Taking the example of a car once again, a buyer might consider the safety features to be the most relevant, both from a personal viewpoint and from that of the buyer's family (personal protection is a benefit). Wearing a 'business hat', the same buyer might also prioritise the extent to which the vehicle will impress colleagues and customers.

In their selection and use, benefits must be matched appropriately to the customer's situation and needs.

PRESENTING THE BEST CASE

MAKING IT ATTRACTIVE

BENEFITS AND FEATURES (Cont'd)

Benefits are what customers want to hear about, but the fact that something **is** a benefit does not make it irresistible or negate the need to add attractiveness in other ways.

Benefits must be well described in order to add power to the case.

Description needs precision and must be well matched to the individual customer. Saying something is 'sort of shiny' is vague and paints no real picture compared with saying, for instance, 'it is as smooth as silk'.

Example

A grill might be described as having a cooking area of so many square millimetres (a technical feature) or as being of a size suitable to grill six steaks at the same time. The latter is a benefit, is truly descriptive and easily conjures up an accurate picture and representation of the size.

PRESENTING THE BEST CASE

DIFFERENTIATING FROM COMPETITION

Benefits build a case and, potentially, build a stronger case than that of the competition. Two factors are especially important here:

- **How** things are described (the power of the point made)
- The **cumulative** effect (a number of minor benefits can outweigh a competitor's major benefit, making all the difference)

Example

Company 'A' is the market leader and this alone may give it an advantage. Other companies cannot combat this directly since, by definition, there is only one market leader. But several other advantages or benefits - eg: the technical merits of the product/service or delivery or backup - can cumulatively outweigh one major advantage.

It is a question of analysing and orchestrating the case you make to ensure its impact mounts up progressively.

DIFFERENTIATING FROM COMPETITION

A well-presented case achieves a great deal. A case that is also tailored to an individual customer achieves still more.

Tailoring a case links back to the process of identifying needs and questioning techniques. You need to match your case to the information that you obtained. Make it obvious to the customers that you are *selecting* what to say and how to say it just for them. Do this by:

- Remembering what they said and how they said it
- Attributing your comments to them; for example, say *You said this had to be cost effective, so…*(and describing how it is) rather than just saying *This is cost effective…*
- Matching your tone and content to their situation (if they emphasised something, reflect this in your case)
- Describing what you do say as tailored; for instance: *Now, because you said timing was so important, let me take that next…*

The more your customers feel you are dealing with them, and not just 'working from a script', the more they will see you as different from the competition.

PRESENTING THE BEST CASE

DIFFERENTIATING FROM COMPETITION

You can use precise aspects of your manner to augment the feeling of individuality you create with a customer.

Use aspects of the 'professional approach' (mentioned earlier) to augment the personal touch you bring to bear. Do this, for example, by:

- Stressing how knowledgeable you are, when this will give reassurance
- Displaying confidence, when you need to combat doubt
- Giving attention to detail, when the customer wants to dot every i and cross every t
- Talking about the future relationship, when for instance the customer is concerned about ongoing service

The way you do this, combined with the way in which you relate to the information that the customer provided earlier, creates a style and approach that are likely to be seen as different from – and better than – that of the competition. Just one well-chosen detail here can transform the way you are seen – and how your case is taken on board.

SELLING THE PRICE

Price is an area of core product/service description to be dealt with positively.

The job is not to <u>defend</u> price, so much as demonstrate value for money (being cheap is rarely a virtue).

Find ways of describing the price that actively build value for money. One way is to use the arithmetic signs as prompts to descriptive phraseology:

+ This plus.../in addition to...

− Reducing costs.../eliminating the need for.../lessening...

X Multiple advantages.../enhanced.../greater.../more.../several...

÷ Amortise costs over.../spread across.../divided between.../apportioned to...

PRESENTING THE BEST CASE

MAKING IT CREDIBLE

If you are selling, customers see you as having an axe to grind; say something is good and they react by thinking: 'Well, they would say that, wouldn't they'. Fair enough.

A credible case may need to contain proof, evidence from a source other than the salesperson.

The following all add credibility:

- Results of research
- Testimonials of existing or past customers (or even just a mention of them)
- Standards (particularly those set by statutory or official bodies)
- Tests or demonstrations (see for yourself)
- The power of numbers (eg: 100,000 sold, 20 years' experience)

You need to match such factors to your own product or service.

PRESENTING THE BEST CASE

MAKING IT CREDIBLE
PROOF

Evidence or proof can be added either specifically or generally. For example:

Specific proof might be added (in the case of the car, once again) by saying: 'A test carried out by the Automobile Association recorded 45 miles per gallon in mixed use'.

General proof might be added by saying: 'This model has been on the market for several years and we have sold many thousands of units'.

They are both different in nature, but both add to the feeling of the case being credible. Moreover, the effect is cumulative: what often works best is a series of statements mixing specific and general points together.

Successful salespeople use sufficient proof to make sure potential buyers see their case as truly credible.

PRESENTING THE BEST CASE

MAKING IT CREDIBLE

BE SELECTIVE

Any factor chosen to enhance your case by adding credibility must be well selected so that it is right for the individual customer.

Example

A testimonial from another customer must be from one comparable with the customer to whom you are selling. Pick one from a company that is significantly larger or smaller, or is operating in a completely different industry, then this testimonial will add nothing to your case and, worse, may even detract from it.

"Ah, just the suit I'm looking for"

While some evidence is of general value, the most powerful case is made by selecting just the right things to mention to a particular customer.

ORGANISING THE PRESENTATION

The normal rules of good communication apply throughout the sales process. People find it easier to follow and build up a picture if what is said has:

- A **sound logic** (which may need to be spelled out)

- A **clear sequence** (linking different parts of the message together and, perhaps, usefully flagging ahead what will be done: 'Let me run through something about the specification, the performance and, of course, the cost. First, the...'

- Evidence of having been **well considered** (ie: it sounds as if you have given thought to the best way - for the customer - of putting it across)

A clear, well organised, presentation is most likely to persuade.

PRESENTING THE BEST CASE

AUGMENTING WHAT YOU SAY

1. SALES AIDS

However powerful your presentation, however descriptive, it may need to be enhanced with more than what you say. One way is to use **sales aids**.

There is a plethora of aids, from photographs to graphs, samples to models. In using them:

- Introduce them and explain how your showing them will help the customer: 'You will see the relationship immediately on this pie chart...'

- Let the customer look at them uninterrupted; this means keeping quiet and waiting

- Do not interrupt; let them decide how long to give it

- Only move on in the discussion when their attention returns to you, emphasising what the aid will have shown them before moving on to the next topic

- At that point remove the sales aid so that it does not distract (though say if you intend to leave something with them at the end of the meeting)

AUGMENTING WHAT YOU SAY

2. DEMONSTRATION

If you have to physically demonstrate your product in action, then:

- Be prepared and set up fast in a way that appears organised and efficient
- Make what you do understandable (logic and structure are important here)
- Make it work - first time and 100%
- Make it make them feel **they** could do it (indeed part of the demonstration may involve them doing just that)
- Emphasise key issues (eg: quality, ease, cost-effectiveness) as you go
- Offer proof where appropriate
- Maintain interest (keep talking when you have to go through stages that are of less interest than others)
- Do not try to compete with any interruptions

And demonstrate benefits when describing the results of the exercise rather than just the exercise itself; make it impressive.

USE ANYTHING NECESSARY TO ADD TO YOUR CASE RATHER THAN SOLELY RELYING ON WHAT YOU SAY.

CHECKING UNDERSTANDING

It is easy to get the bit between your teeth at this stage of the sales process. You are off to a good start, the prospect is clearly interested but the danger is that you find yourself on 'automatic pilot', going through the case you wish to make without a break.

It is important to **check progress as you go**, not only to ensure your customers are understanding and 'with you so far', but also to ensure they like what you're saying; it provides an opportunity for them to have a say and makes them feel you are directing your commentary just for them.

How? Simply by pausing to ask check questions occasionally as you go: 'How does that sound? Is that clear? Would it be useful to give you more detail about that?'

Keep customers' attention and ensure they are 'with you' throughout the meeting; provide an opportunity for them to participate as appropriate.

PRESENTING THE BEST CASE

SUMMARY

This is the core of the sales meeting and probably takes up the majority of the time involved. To be persuasive you must:

- Match the case you make to the individual customer
- Select and present an appropriate amount of detail (customers are busy; comprehensiveness is rarely an objective; customers not salespeople dictate the amount of detail necessary)
- Make the case proceed fluently and in a well organised fashion
- Maintain two-way communication and encourage feedback where appropriate
- And always make sure that what you do comes over as 'for them', not as the standard approach or description you use for every customer

Make it understandable, attractive and credible and it will differentiate you from the competition and act to persuade.

NOTES

HANDLING OBJECTIONS

HANDLING OBJECTIONS

WHY THEY OCCUR

Objections are a natural part of the buying process, of weighing up and trying to identify the best deal. Buyers want to:

- Consider the pluses and minuses alongside each other

- Take (and often be seen to take) a considered view

- Get the salesperson talking about specifics (that are not necessarily part of the planned presentation)

- Include a judgement about how objections are handled, as part of their assessment of both the individual and what is being offered for sale

Do not be surprised by objections. They are inherent to the selling - and buying - process; handling them 'goes with the territory'.

THE OPPORTUNITY

You need to view objections positively.

The first rules are to:

- Regard them as a sign of interest (after all, why would anyone ask anything about something they had totally rejected?)

- Anticipate and, perhaps, pre-empt them (you will quickly get to know the main matters that are raised regularly)

- Never let conversations about objections descend into arguments: 'It's very expensive... No, it isn't... Well, I think it is...'

- Think back and reinforce your case if necessary (objections may arise because you have neglected to fully explain something earlier in the conversation)

Remember, handling objections well can say something about you, boosting your image and reinforcing credibility.

HANDLING OBJECTIONS

A TWO-STAGE APPROACH

STAGE 1

Before an objection can be answered it must be **acknowledged.** Jumping in, especially with a denial, gives quite the wrong impression and tends to lead to an adversarial situation and to argument.

An acknowledgement (which may only be a few words: 'That's certainly something we need to review... Yes, that's a fair point, let me give you some more background') will:

● Indicate to your customers that you believe they have a point

● Show that you are not going to argue

● Make it clear that you are likely to respond with something serious and considered (including 'yes' in the acknowledgement may help)

● Give you a moment to think (something you may welcome or even seek to extend: 'Let me think about that for a second')

Good acknowledgement makes subsequent handling of objections more straightforward.

A TWO-STAGE APPROACH

STAGE 2

The range of approaches to handling objections is limited, you can either:

- Remove them

- Reduce their power and significance

- Change them into something seen as positive

- Agree that they represent a snag

All these are, in effect, re-balancing the pluses and minuses.

Remember, it is the overall vision of the balance on which a decision to buy is made, and a small difference can act to create a winning balance.

HANDLING OBJECTIONS

EMPHASISE THE POSITIVE

The approach you take to handling an objection will work best if it focuses on the positive side as well as dealing with the negative.

Example
If you take the line of aiming to reduce the buyer's perception of the severity of a snag, then link it to positive factors to emphasise the total balance: 'Of course, the model with the 5-speed gearbox is more expensive; however the difference is small compared with the saving on fuel costs and...'

In the words of the Hitchhikers' Guide to the Galaxy: DON'T PANIC. Sensitive handling of the objections buyers raise acts to build your case and enhances the impression you make and the credibility you achieve.

CLOSING SUCCESSFULLY

WHY IT IS NECESSARY

Closing is an important stage, though one that may be very brief. It is here that a commitment can be tied down, but it must be seen - and used - in the right light.

Closing does not cause people to buy; it is the whole process of building a persuasive case that has now been done that does that. Closing converts the interest you have generated during the meeting into action - that of agreeing an order.

THE DANGER

The greatest danger of this stage of the sales process is not that closing will be done badly, but that it will not be done at all.

It is very easy to find you are avoiding the close (it is at this point, after all, that you can get a 'yes' or a 'no'). What happens is that the final elements of making your case are continued beyond a point when this is helpful: 'Right, I hope this has been useful; is there anything else I can tell you?' The customer can then take control: 'This really has been most useful. I am sure that I have all the detail I need. Thank you for taking so much trouble...goodbye'.

Beware: it is possible to receive a pleasant and positive response, but lose control and then be unable to close at all.

CLOSING SUCCESSFULLY

WHEN TO CLOSE

Simplistically, the rule is: close as soon as you can.

What this really means is that, once you are convinced the buyer has sufficient information to make a decision, and that the overall picture (balance) is positive and able to do the persuasion job required, you can close.

Judge when the time is right by watching for **buying signals.** These are signs that the buyer is ready to make the decision, eg:

- Reference to the product/service in use (by them)
- Questions about post-purchase details (installation, results that follow, etc)

Successful salespeople plan to close, prepare to close and are prepared to close.

CLOSING SUCCESSFULLY

THE TRIAL CLOSE

The ultimate way to prompt a buying signal is to use a trial close.

This is where you close early on, even at a stage when you are pretty sure the answer will be 'no', but with the intention of obtaining clues as to the best way forward.

Example

You say something like: 'Well, let's go ahead. Can I organise six for you?'. The response is immediate: 'Hang on, we aren't at that stage yet! What about the payment terms? This is a big investment you know'.

You abandon the close and equally immediately move into a discussion about payment terms. You now know what the key final point is, and something more about how the customer feels about it.

With a meeting that is going well, a trial close may present no real risk and be a good route to a speedy conclusion.

CLOSING METHODS

So, how do you actually execute the close? Methods vary, but all have the same objective and all must be matched to the circumstances: the kind of customer you are dealing with and the character of the meeting that is taking place.

Methods include:

- **Direct request.** Just a straightforward question: 'Shall we go ahead? How much would you like? When shall we start?' Or, perhaps, one linked to the plus side of the balance: 'When can we start getting the improvements we have discussed?'

- **Command.** With some customers you can virtually tell them to commit: 'Let's get this organised; let me have written confirmation and I will put matters in hand...'

- **Immediate gain.** This offers a reason for deciding now, rather than later: 'If you give me the go ahead now, then I can have it up and running by the end of the month'. Other factors offered as immediate gain include financial savings, additional guarantees and specific people being involved (with services).

CLOSING METHODS

- **Fear close.** This reverses the immediate gain close, putting it on an 'unless' basis: 'If you are not able to give me the go-ahead today, that deadline is really going to cause problems'.

- **Alternatives.** What is called a 'yes or yes' question: 'Would you like 10 or 20? Do you want to schedule this for this month or next month?' In other words, whichever alternative is agreed produces an order.

- **Summary.** This suits situations where the case you make is complex. It links a brief recap of key factors (or benefits) with a simple closing statement or question: 'So, this gives you something easy to install, that will work well with your existing equipment and that your staff can be quickly briefed to operate. Can we go ahead?'

- **Assumption.** This literally assumes the customer will say 'yes' and continues the conversation as if this has actually happened: 'Right, we seem to be agreed. Let me get the documentation sorted and we can go on from there'.

Complexity of technique is often unnecessary here; if what has been done previously has been effective, then closing can be a detail. **But, always close and always do it confidently and positively.**

NOTES

FOLLOW-UP ACTIVITY

LEAVING NO STONE UNTURNED

Some sales are concluded in one meeting that ends with the customer saying 'yes'. Others are more complex and demand additional action and techniques to tie down the sale.

The key objective here is to increase the strike rate.

At the close, no area of business enjoys 100% agreement. If the customer fails to agree, the task is to take additional action, where possible, to retrieve the situation and turn a negative position into a positive one. Inevitably, this will not always work. But, add an additional rate of strike here to those where agreement is more easily reached, and the total success rate becomes more worthwhile.

Successful salespeople always pursue every possibility of achieving a positive result.

DEALING WITH HESITATION

Once you close, customers may respond with those ominous words: 'I'll think about it' (ie: neither a 'yes' nor a 'no'). What do you do?

- Always agree: 'Of course, it's an important decision and you must be sure...'

- But check, asking why it is necessary: 'But, do you say that for any particular reason? Are there details that you are not sure about?'

This allows you to focus on any points that are then raised ('Well, I suppose it's mainly the question of...') and then to continue the conversation, after which it may well be possible to close again.

This technique can directly increase the ratio of success.

PERSISTENCE

Persistence is the simplest technique available to increase the ratio of success. Some sales go, quite simply, to those who refuse to give up.

FOLLOW-UP ACTIVITY

PERSISTENCE

THE PROBLEM

Follow-up can be difficult, though the problem is largely psychological. You start with good intentions but when you have made three telephone calls in a week and on each occasion you are greeted by a secretary saying 'Sorry, they're in a meeting', paranoia sets in. You see them in your mind's eye saying, 'Tell them I'm not here'.

Recognising the problem is the first step to overcoming it.

It may help to remember that the hard work is done at this stage. It is surely easier to make one more follow-up call to tie something down, rather that let it go by default, find a new prospect and go through the whole sales process again.

Persistence produces greater productivity and more positive sales results.

FOLLOW-UP ACTIVITY

PERSISTENCE

GUIDELINES

In following up, it pays to:

- Take what is said at face value

- Try and agree a time when it is appropriate/possible to get in touch again

- Bear in mind that the customer's need to buy may be less urgent than your need to secure an order (yes, really!)

- Keep in touch (if your customers really have no interest they will eventually stop making excuses and tell you straight)

Remember, some orders come because you are thick-skinned enough to make one more contact than a competitor.

PERSISTENCE

VARYING THE METHODS

Often the prime method for this kind of follow-up is to telephone. But, a telephone call may come at a genuinely bad moment for the customer (when his or her mind is on other priorities) and it leaves no record.

So, vary the follow-up method, eg:

- Write a short letter
- Send something out (new information, press coverage about the product/service, more detail)
- Send a fax (this still seems to imply a degree of urgency though the copy received is not so visibly impressive as a letter on printed stationery)

Mix these forms of contact with telephone calls when appropriate.

Take care: e-mail may be easy (particularly for you) but it is not ideal as the only means of follow-up sales communication. Remember, it is all too easy to wipe it off screen and forget it at the touch of a button.

DEVELOPING REPEAT BUSINESS

There is an old maxim to the effect that business will only continue to flow as long as you are remembered. And memories are short. Moreover, there are all too many competitors intent on filling any gap you leave.

The moral: business is too important to be allowed to go by default. When you have done the groundwork, secured the first order and fulfilled it successfully - creating a satisfied customer - it is a waste not to build on that success.

To create chances for repeat business you must:

- **Keep in touch**
- **Watch for and create opportunities**
- **Maintain service and quality standards**

DEVELOPING NEW BUSINESS
SELLING THE RANGE

Many organisations have a range of products. Sales opportunities and results are increased if customers can be persuaded to buy more than one product/service.

True sales excellence includes the ability to cross sell.

A simple manifestation of this is what is often called 'gin and tonic' selling: when customers go into the off-licence for a bottle of spirits, the sales assistants (if they are on the ball) will say as a reflex, 'How many mixers do you want?'

So, you should:

- Make the link(s) that work in your business
- Use and mention the links
- Sell the two (or more) things in parallel, so that each supports and enhances the other

NOTES

SUMMARY

ALLIED SKILLS

1. NUMERACY

Sales success does not just happen. The chances of success can be increased through the way selling is conducted.

Selling demands planning, preparation and attention to detail. It also demands the deployment of a plethora of skills and techniques that, together, can create a truly persuasive yet customer-orientated approach.

In addition to traditional selling skills, four allied skills are key:

1. Numeracy
Because selling results in people buying something - and paying for it - the financial elements of the sale are vital. Negotiation, demanding a range of techniques that go beyond selling, may be involved. Certainly, salespeople must increasingly have, and display, an ability with figures or their credibility, and ability to ensure profitability, are always going to be in doubt.

ALLIED SKILLS

2. PRESENTATION

Many sales situations demand not only skills to be deployed in a face-to-face meeting, but also the skills of formal presentation.

Sales success may depend on being just as credible and persuasive in a formal, group situation as in a one-to-one meeting.

From the customers' perspective, presentational performance is used as an additional judgemental element in weighing up a case. People do not say: 'What excellent ideas, shame it was not better presented'. Instead, they say: 'What a poor presentation, I don't expect the ideas are much good either'. This is not unfair; it is life.

Successful salespeople cultivate presentational skills and ensure they are as persuasive 'on their feet' as in a meeting.

ALLIED SKILLS

3. PERSUASIVE WRITING

The same principle as applies to presentation is important here. An increasing amount of sales contact must be in writing: sales letters, seemingly simple follow-up communications, detailed written proposals - all are important.

Further, because much time and effort may have been invested to get a contact to the stage of wanting, say, a proposal, if the standard of written communication is not sufficiently high to carry things forward all that has gone before is wasted.

If the basic content and linguistic style of your writing fails to facilitate cognition in a comprehensive...

Sorry, start again! **No gobbledegook, no office-speak. Your writing must be as clear, easy to follow and persuasive as what you say, while also projecting some style and personality that says something about you.**

Note: even informal communication, like e-mail, must look good and read well.

ALLIED SKILLS

4. ACCOUNT MANAGEMENT

Selling is not a one off, isolated occasion or exercise. You may aim to go on doing business with a customer, perhaps on an increasing scale, for weeks, months or years.

Therefore, the ongoing relationship requires attention. You need to give thought to:

- Creating an appropriate relationship (one the customer feels is suitable)
- Managing the ongoing process (from analysing the opportunities to maintaining regular contact)
- Holding the account and developing customer loyalty
- Developing the potential for increased business in the future

If sales creates customers, rather than simply orders, it will work better in the long-term.

CUSTOMER FOCUS

A theme throughout the techniques reviewed here has been that of focusing on the customer. To recap: selling is best regarded as the process that assists customers to make buying decisions. Further, customers are wary; they do not want to be pushed. They see the salesperson as someone with an axe to grind.

So, success is made most likely by:

- Having and displaying an understanding of customers
- Identifying and using information about customer needs
- Communicating in a way that tells customers what they want to know rather than what you want to tell them
- Making what is done individual, manifestly tailored to the individual customer

CUSTOMERS' PET HATES

Understanding customers also means appreciating the kind of things they do not like and which dilute persuasiveness. Such include:

- Not getting to the point promptly
- Being too abrupt
- Talking too much
- Asking too few questions
- Not listening
- Being, or appearing to be, inadequately prepared
- Interrupting the customer
- Lacking confidence or conviction
- Pressurising the customer

Or, looking scruffy, moaning about the market and... so on and so on.

Sensitivity to customers is key to sales success.

SUMMARY

REMAIN FLEXIBLE

In a sense, selling is as much an art as a science. Understanding the techniques, experience and planning all help but they do not guarantee success. Nor do they imply the possibility of certainty about what will happen in a meeting.

If your methodology becomes locked into one inflexible way of handling things, you make yourself vulnerable.

Remember:

- You cannot **know** in advance how customers will respond
- While there is a repetitive element to selling, responses may surprise: a usually minor matter proves vitally important to a customer or something is said in a way you have not experienced before

If you expect to be surprised, if you avoid standardised responses and proceed thoughtfully and remain ever-flexible to the unexpected, you are more likely to impress and succeed.

A MAGIC FORMULA?

So, at the end of the day is there a magic formula that guarantees sales success? Sadly the answer must be 'no'. There are simply too many variables - not least the fickle nature of customers - and too much detail involved for that to be possible.

However, from an overall perspective, you might dwell on the points listed on the following page. Together, they come about as close to a magic formula as exists.

From this, you can see that selling is not repetitive; rather, it is a constant challenge and a process that can bring regular satisfaction and reward.

SUMMARY

A MAGIC FORMULA?

Excellence in selling tends to go not to those with some inbuilt predisposition to be persuasive, but to those who:

- Understand the sales process and how it works

- Understand the psychology of their customers and how they make buying decisions

- Study, concentrate on and deploy the various sales techniques available as appropriate for them and for their customers

- Tailor their approach: running the kind of meeting that is best for each individual customer today (not giving everyone the standard spiel or becoming locked into an 'automatic pilot' way of working that precludes tailoring the approach)

- Recognise that selling is a dynamic process (that what is right for one customer today may not be right tomorrow) and, therefore, see fine-tuning their approach as a continual necessity

A FINAL WORD

While it is always a thrill when a customer says 'yes', remember:

● Sales success is not a matter of good luck (though you might perhaps regard that as the reason why your competitors are successful!)

● The best salespeople work at it and make it happen

After all, if it was too easy, it would be less fun.

About the Author

Patrick Forsyth

Patrick runs Touchstone Training & Consultancy, an independent firm specialising in work in marketing, sales and communications skills. He began his career in publishing – selling books – and then worked for a professional management institute before going into consultancy. He has more than twenty years' experience as a consultant working with organisations in a wide range of industries and many different parts of the world.

In addition to training he writes extensively on business matters – books, articles and training materials. As well as being the author of other Pocketbooks (see opposite) he has a number of other successful business books published. These include *Powerful Reports and Proposals, Marketing on a Tight Budget, The Management Speakers Handbook, Successful Time Management* and *Detox your Career.*

Contact

Patrick can be contacted at:
Touchstone Training & Consultancy
28 Saltcote Maltings, Maldon, Essex CM9-4QP
Tel/fax: 01621-859300
E-mail: patrick@touchstonetc.freeserve.co.uk

COMPLEMENTARY TITLES

Patrick Forsyth has written five other Pocketbooks, including *The Starting in Management Pocketbook*, *The Managing Upwards Pocketbook* and *The Meetings Pocketbook*. He has also written:

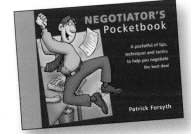

The Negotiator's Pocketbook, valuable to all in selling. It reviews the techniques involved in negotiating terms and making the best deal. One reviewer said of this:
A very practical book, not just giving you the key principles, but full of tips which can help you feel like an expert and negotiate with confidence.

Hook your audience, a collection of stories, quotations, quips, proverbs, sayings and miscellaneous words of wit and wisdom for those who need to enliven a meeting, conference or training session.

Other titles in the series particularly relevant to sales people include:

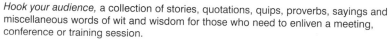

- *The Key Account Manager's Pocketbook*
- *The Salesperson's Pocketbook*
- *The Telesales Pocketbook*
- *The Marketing Pocketbook*

- *The International Trade Pocketbook*
- *The Customer Service Pocketbook*
- *The Cultural Gaffes Pocketbook*
- *The E-commerce Pocketbook*

ORDER FORM

Your details

Name _____

Position _____

Company _____

Address _____

_____

Telephone _____

Facsimile _____

E-mail _____

VAT No. (EC companies) _____

Your Order Ref _____

Please send me:

		No. copies
The Sales Excellence	Pocketbook	[ ]
The _____	Pocketbook	[ ]
The _____	Pocketbook	[ ]
The _____	Pocketbook	[ ]
The _____	Pocketbook	[ ]

Order by Post

MANAGEMENT POCKETBOOKS LTD
LAUREL HOUSE, STATION APPROACH, ALRESFORD,
HAMPSHIRE SO24 9JH UK

Order by Phone, Fax or Internet

Telephone: +44 (0)1962 735573
Facsimile: +44 (0)1962 733637
E-mail: sales@pocketbook.co.uk
Web: www.pocketbook.co.uk

Customers in USA should contact:
Stylus Publishing, LLC, 22883 Quicksilver Drive,
Sterling, VA 20166-2012
Telephone: 703 661 1581 or 800 232 0223
Facsimile: 703 661 1501 E-mail: styluspub@aol.com